BE WISE BE OTHERWISE

KEVIN MACNEIL lives on Skye and is an award-winning writer of poetry and prose. He was born and raised on the Isle of Lewis and is the inaugural recipient of the Iain Crichton Smith Bilingual Writing Fellowship (Writer in Residence for the Highlands area). His first poetry collection won the prestigious Tivoli Europa Giovani International Poetry Prize (2000). MacNeil frequently collaborates with artists and musicians and is a founder member of the trip-hop poetry band Tommorrowscope. His work has been translated into ten languages.

By the same author

Love and Zen in the Outer Hebrides,
Canongate Books, 1998
Wish I Was Here, ed. by Kevin MacNeil and
Alec Finlay, Pocketbooks, 2000
Baile Beag Gun Chriochran/A Little Borderless Village,
ed. by Kevin MacNeil, Highland Council, 2000

BE WISE

BE

OTHER WISE

*Ideas and advice for your
kind of person*

KEVIN MACNEIL

CANONGATE

For

*Krungthepmahanakhornbowornrattanakosinmahint
arayutthayamahadilokpopnopparatratchathaniburiro
mudomratchaniwetmahasathanamornpimanavatarns
athitsakkathattiyavisnukarprasit*

&

the one who knows why

First published in Great Britain in 2001 by
Canongate Books Ltd,
14 High Street Edinburgh EH1 1TE

10 9 8 7 6 5 4 3 2 1

Copyright © Kevin MacNeil, 2001

The publishers gratefully acknowledge subsidy
from the Scottish Arts Council towards the publication of this volume

British Library Cataloguing-in-Publication Data
A catalogue record for this book is available on
request from the British Library

ISBN 1 84195 110 2

Typeset by Forge Design
Printed and bound by
Omnia Books Limited, Glasgow

Remember what things were like for you
before you were born.

At least once in a while, have a mountaintop under your feet.

Sometimes there are answers for which there are just no questions.

Remember to wake up like you've never woken up before.

Have presence.
Give.

Shock culture.

Take an interesting photograph of a boring
object.

Stab yourself in the back. Now that you know what it's like, stop doing it to other people.

Mime your innocence to a CCTV camera.

Earn your demands, that you may demand
what you've earned.

Do you have a job?
Or does a job have you?

Write between the lines.

A river runs through it.
Go fish.

Keeping your old partner, learn a new dance.

Don't live in the past.
(Because you can't.)

Blank out words in promotional signs.

thank you   you

=

come again   again

Purify.

Eat each meal as though it is your first and last.

Keep Britain tiny.

Eternity pivots on now and therefore on you.

If you must be superstitious, make up your own superstitions. Spread them.

Have a good laugh at your passport photo.

Design your own constellations.

Drop in.

Investigate the love-lives of people who had ideas centuries before their time.

Publish without being damned.

Invent a stamp for faxes.

Cast off.

Make a pilgrimage to a zen garden.

Change accents as you would change fonts.

Treat objects as people.

Rearrange your diary.
Begin the year with July.

The unsuitable will sometimes suit.

Even a sock needs a partner.

Write your autobiography, not your cv.

Don't be scared of absence, even if it follows
you around.

Here, of all places, right now – you.
You who once set out naked and daft.

Pool focus.

Obliterate sarcasm with a healthy chuckle.

Correspond.
Make correspondences.

Step into the same river twice.

Believe in aliens but not in dinosaurs.

Commit random acts of art.

Decide, but not now.

Now.

Don't be a zen-ophobic.

Recognise the new.

Speak easy.

Also remember people for what they didn't do.

It matters little to Neophron Percnopterus, the Egyptian Vulture, that its more common name is shite-hawk.

You can take a seahorse to water.

Find out what everyone in your first primary
school class is now doing.

Devote time to considering your final answer.

Understand
the point of contact.

Because it's free does not mean you can afford it.

Should old quaintness be forgot?

Define your approach to freedom cagily.

Consider the frame before that which is contained.

If leaving a job, bring board games to work on
your last day.

Include Others.

You must remember this: you don't need a good memory.

A warm hug is a comfort, though not always so in the case of mistaken identity.

Let flattery fall flat.

Your dreams form one enormous jigsaw.

Grasp. But never physically.

Don't sigh when you feel contentment.

Compare where you've been with where you haven't.

Adopt a sister, a brother.

Waters still run deep.

Not all the best tunes have been written, and maybe not all the best times have been had.

Visit a city you know nothing about.

Insist a cliché is just a proverb's poverty-stricken cousin.

Learn an obscure language, keep it alive.

Exaggerate your understatements.

A simple kiss can shock.

Read to a child.
(But be careful what you read.)

Make. Do.

Take a story for a walk.
(Remove the leash.)

There are so many people in the world that
the chances of someone breathing in absolute
unison with you right now are very high
indeed.
Feel synchronised.

Define what it means to know a person.

Celebrate when you want to, not because you have to.

Your own values make you valuable.

Memorise those words you would wish to be your last.

Spend the day closely imitating your favourite soap opera character.

Go to a large library and read the most unusual book you can find.

As a spokesman for people of your kind, have something to say.

Try whispering it.
Try shouting it.
Try re-writing it.

Read a contemporary teenage novel.

Buy loads of presents and distribute them on your birthday.

Wonder at the sea.

Indulge in diversions.
Throw away the road map.

Still be.

Carve your tattoo on a tree.

If you like staying inside, move home.

Reincarnate the environment.

Change the face of graffiti.

Visit the birth places of your ten favourite writers.

Create atmosphere.

Encourage the use of mistletoe.

Ask the oldest person you know what it's all
about.

There's no need to kill time.

Make a list of those words you don't like. Burn it
and never use those words again.

Context is all,
all is context.

Collect driftwood, make artpieces,
throw them back.

You are already adequately equipped.

Adjust your sleep pattern to give it a hypnotically beautiful shape.

Get a yen for zen.

Even misery loves company.

Hold a shoe to your ear.
Hear the footsteps?

Turn the tv off.
Watch an aquarium instead.

Don't be scared of reading.
Don't be scared of writing.

Stand with those who withstand.

Visit an art gallery.
Take home themes from your own life.

Dial a random phone number and quote from this book.

From today, believe in the mirror and not in the fashion magazines.

Imagine your parents as they were when they first met.

Write a haiku, replacing the season word with an obscenity.

Tell a bilingual joke.
It doesn't have to be funny.

Try and recall the ongoing events of a single day of primary school, from the first bell until last.

Consider: if you were interrogated, what would it take to make you blurt?

And re-lax.

Illustrate what you mean.

And send those illustrations to your local newspaper.

Use an archaic word until you're so sick of it
you never want to hear it again.

Misquote yourself.

Imagine all the people.

Re-signal your train of thought.

Consider the inanity of shouting at other
cars, the tv, computers . . .
And do it anyway.

Have the courage to doubt the sacrifices you make.

Pore over old photographs without the indulgence of regret.

Put wise statements before bank statements.

Play like each note is your last.

Remember. Taking a risk is about more than going to the toilet without locking the door.

An afterlife?
You don't deserve one if you can't think of
what to do on a rainy afternoon.

Appreciate brief longings.

Recommend the things you love to the people you love.

Open your eyes like the sun rising.

Once in a while, indulge in the power to confuse.

Never admit guilt.
'It was all in the name of performance art.'

Keep your spirit level.

Make a speech that will change someone's life.

Leave this world penniless and barefoot.

Maxim-ise.

Don't pursue trivia because – what then?

Pay for your lottery tickets with forged notes. Then give the money you would have spent on tickets to the charities of your choice.

Set a pop song to intelligent lyrics.
Sing this version at karaoke.

Employ a decoy.

Develop an instinct for developing instincts.

When someone inadvertently makes a quip and says, 'No pun intended!' look them straight in the eye and say with a grimace, 'That's all right. None achieved.'

Take it easy.
But do take it.

Enjoy casual movement.

Campaign to protect an endangered species –
the ugliest one you can find.

Cherish.

It takes one to trust one.

Forget that snow is plain old water.

Be generous with your time.
It's free.

Nothing is definitive.

Roam the spectrum freely.

Improve your favourites.

Pinpoint your thoughts on apathy.

Repeat things only when you must. (Repeat things.)

Don't go off the rails; unless you accept the rails were there in the first place.

Experiment with your social skills.

Consider the ghillies.

Where you are is never the periphery.

Don't lose confidence.
Lose arrogance.

Improvise inaccurate weather rhymes.

Will power is free, free will is power.

Sanctify a place no one else holds dear.

Write your own elegy, code it, and bury it in the text of your will.

Forget what you didn't want to know.

What's the fuss?

Do exercise as you see fit.

Solve a crime that occurred centuries ago.

Appreciate it while it's there.

Buy shares.
Share.

Your life, as well as your death, should make
a difference.
But one is more meaningful.

Start a stop-watch craze.
Wear an egg-timer on your wrist.

Consider the reason most western men in the 30s, 40s and 50s wore hats.

Define your motives.

The necessary isn't necessarily so.

Don't just be honest.
Be honest, but be just.

Without consulting any kind of map, atlas, or related source, draw freehand a map of your country.
Now add the rivers.
And streams.

Send a letter of thanks (or commiseration) to someone who has influenced you.

After a visit to the doctor/dentist/hospital,
buy yourself a present.

Become intimate friends with somebody
much richer and somebody much poorer than
you.
Introduce them with verve.

Be a super human.

(Shrug.
It's a zeitgeist thing.)